The NEW COVENANT JOURNEY

THE BASIC GOSPEL STUDY SERIES
CONNECTING YOU TO
THE LOVE OF JESUS CHRIST

THE NEW COVENANT JOURNEY

Copyright © 2014 Basic Gospel, Inc., Lewisville, TX 75057
ISBN 978-1-931-899-38-3

Printed in the United States of America.

Contents

INTRODUCTION

If God had a will, would you be listed as a beneficiary? If so, what would you inherit?

Here is the short answer. If you have trusted Jesus Christ, you are an heir of God and a joint heir with Jesus Christ (see Romans 8:17).

But what does that mean, and how does this astonishing news affect you here and now?

It changes everything. As the Bible says, "All things have become new." (2 Corinthians 5:17)

- A new relationship with God is yours through the love and grace of Jesus Christ.
- A new identity is yours based on God's specific promise.
- A new way of life is yours because the Holy Spirit lives within you.
- A new purpose is yours because you rest in Jesus' finished work.

The New Covenant, or God's legal will, provides everything you need for your journey as a believer in Christ. God desires that you embrace all that is yours and experience to the full the New Covenant Life.

There is nothing that can compare to it. So let's begin. Let's take an in-depth look at God's will and what this wonderful covenant has in store for you.

CHAPTER ONE

God's Will, Your Benefits
PART ONE

God has a will for your life. If you are like most people, you want to know what that will is. You want to know the plan God has for you — who you will marry, where you will live, what you will do in life. These are good questions, but they reveal a limited, self-focused perspective. Let's shift gears and think about God's will from his perspective.

A will in our culture constitutes a legal document that lays out what happens at a person's death. It is the same with God's will. When Jesus died, God's will took effect. All the provisions are contained within what the Bible calls the New Covenant. As we will see, God has provided everything you will ever need to experience life to the full. Paul was so taken by this New Covenant he devoted his life to introducing others to their inheritance in Jesus Christ. Through this study you will learn of your inheritance.

As you participate in this study, please keep these points in mind. The New Covenant...

- Is God's will for you.
- Is better than the Old Covenant.
- Began at Jesus' death.

THE NEW COVENANT

Before looking at the New Covenant itself we need to understand its importance overall.

> *He has made us competent as ministers of a new covenant—not of the letter but of the Spirit; for the letter kills, but the Spirit gives life.*
> *2 Corinthians 3:6*

1. What does Paul say about the New Covenant in the first part of this passage?

2. Why does he say it? Reread the second half of the passage.

Think about what this means

- There was a covenant which existed before - the Old Covenant.
- That Old Covenant has been replaced by the New Covenant.
- You are to be a minister of this New Covenant.
- You have been made competent to do so by the Holy Spirit.
- A line in the sand has been drawn, a stark contrast – Death in the Old vs. Life in the New.

Something you didn't have has been granted to you, and it has been granted on the basis of God's initiative rather than your abilities; given by grace, not earned by works!

THE PROMISE

God promised the New Covenant through Jeremiah some 600 years before it would become a reality. Upfront, he stated this New Covenant would be different than the Old. This prophecy was so important the writer of Hebrews quoted it directly. Let's take a look.

> *For if there had been nothing wrong with that first covenant, no place would have been sought for another. But God found fault with the people and said: "The time is coming, declares the Lord, when I will make a new covenant with the house of Israel and with the house of Judah. It will not be like the covenant I made with their forefathers when I took them by the hand to lead them out of Egypt, because they did not remain faithful to my covenant, and I turned away from them, declares the Lord. This is the covenant I will make with the house of Israel after that time, declares the Lord. I will put my laws in their minds and write them on their hearts. I will be their God, and they will be my people. No longer will a man teach his neighbor, or a man his brother, saying, 'Know the Lord,' because they will all know me, from the least of them to the greatest. For I will forgive their wickedness and will remember their sins no more. By calling this covenant "new," he has made the first one obsolete; and what is obsolete and aging will soon disappear.*
>
> Hebrews 8:7-13

1. What are the four provisions of the New Covenant?

   a.

   b.

   c.

   d.

2. Pick one word for each provision to describe what it means to you.

   a.

   b.

   c.

   d.

3. By calling this covenant "new", what does God say about the first covenant?

   a.

   b.

4. Who mediates this covenant?

   But the ministry Jesus has received is as superior to theirs as the covenant of which he is mediator is superior to the old one, and it is founded on better promises.

   Hebrews 8:6

5. What change is required because of this covenant?

   For when there is a change of the priesthood, there must also be a change of the law. He of whom these things are said belonged to a different tribe, and no one from that tribe has ever served at the altar. For it is clear that our Lord descended from Judah, and in regard to that tribe Moses said nothing about priests.

   Hebrews 7:12-14

6. Does this covenant provide a means of gaining forgiveness when someone sins?

   And where these have been forgiven, there is no longer any sacrifice for sin.

   Hebrews 10:18

7. What does this say about your forgiveness in Christ?

THE PLACE OF CHANGE

If the New Covenant is better than the Old, something needed to happen in order to move from the first to the second.

1. How was the Mosaic Covenant ratified, or put into effect?

   Moses then took the blood, sprinkled it on the people and said, "This is the blood of the covenant that the Lord has made with you in accordance with all these words."

   Exodus 24:8

2. How and when was the New Covenant ratified, or put into effect?

   How much more, then, will the blood of Christ, who through the eternal Spirit offered himself unblemished to God, cleanse our consciences from acts that lead to death, so that we may serve the living God! For this reason Christ is the mediator of a new covenant, that those who are called may receive the promised eternal inheritance—now that he has died as a ransom to set them free from the sins committed under the first covenant. In the case of a will, it is necessary to prove the death of the one who made it, because a will is in force only when somebody has died; it never takes effect while the one who made it is living.

   Hebrews 9:14-17

3. How many times did this sacrifice take place?

But now he has appeared once for all at the end of the ages to do away with sin by the sacrifice of himself.

Hebrews 9:26b

4. Will Jesus ever die again?

So Christ was sacrificed once to take away the sins of many people; and he will appear a second time, not to bear sin, but to bring salvation to those who are waiting for him.

Hebrews 9:28

JESUS AND THE OLD COVENANT

We need one more piece of information to confirm this change from the Old to the New Covenant. What was Jesus' relationship to the Old Covenant?

1. Did Jesus live within the Old Covenant?

But when the time had fully come, God sent his Son, born of a woman, born under law, to redeem those under law, that we might receive the full rights of sons.

Galatians 4:4, 5

2. What did Jesus claim in relation to the law?

   Do not think that I have come to abolish the Law or the Prophets; I have not come to abolish them but to fulfill them. I tell you the truth, until heaven and earth disappear, not the smallest letter, not the least stroke of a pen, will by any means disappear from the Law until everything is accomplished.

   Matthew 5:17, 18

3. Do you think Jesus fulfilled the law? If yes, how?

4. Did he do what he claimed?

   I have brought you glory on earth by completing the work you gave me to do.

   John 17:4

   When he had received the drink, Jesus said, "It is finished." With that, he bowed his head and gave up his spirit.

   John 19:30

5. What do you think Jesus meant when he said "It is finished"?

Therefore, Jesus' death completed the Old Covenant and ratified the New Covenant. One act dealt with both covenants. In other words, **Jesus is the pivot point between the two covenants.**

In the first part of this overview of the New Covenant we have studied why the New Covenant was necessary, learned the four provisions of this covenant, looked at several key differences between the Old and New Covenants and learned how Jesus fulfilled the Old and ushered in the New. There is much more to come, much more incredibly good news to consider. As preparation for the next chapter, please consider this question: As a believer, which covenant applies to you?

CHAPTER TWO

God's Will, Your Benefits
PART TWO

In the last chapter we explored the importance
of the New Covenant, its definition as the writer
of Hebrews quoted the prophecy from Jeremiah
and how Jesus' death confirmed it. We finished
by asking an important question: As a believer,
which covenant applies to you?

In the second part of this overview of the New Covenant we will
answer this question by looking more closely at the four benefits of
the New Covenant, investigate whether it was limited to Israel and
demonstrate that the Sabbath rest truly is available within it.

FOUR PROMISES

Four amazing promises make up the New Covenant. Let's explore each one.

PROMISE #1

"I will put my laws in their minds and write them on their hearts."
Hebrews 8:10

1. Where were the 10 Commandments written?

   Now if the ministry that brought death, which was engraved in letters on stone, came with glory, so that the Israelites could not look steadily at the face of Moses because of its glory, fading though it was, will not the ministry of the Spirit be even more glorious?
   2 Cor. 3:7, 8

2. In contrast, where does God write the New Covenant laws?

3. Based on the following verses, how did God carry out this promise?

   Therefore, if anyone is in Christ, he is a new creation; the old has gone, the new has come!
   2 Corinthians 5:17

But we have the mind of Christ.

1 Corinthians 2:16b

4. According to this passage, what laws did God write on your heart?

And this is his command: to believe in the name of his Son, Jesus Christ, and to love one another as He commanded us.

1 John 3:23

5. What is another way to describe these laws?

And now these three remain: faith, hope and love. But the greatest of these is love.

1 Corinthians 13:13

6. How are they revealed in your life?

For in Christ Jesus neither circumcision nor uncircumcision has any value. The only thing that counts is faith expressing itself through love.

Galatians 5:6

PROMISE #2

"...I will be their God, and they will be my people."

Hebrews 8:10

1. What does God guarantee us with this promise?

2. How does this promise speak to the issue of assurance of salvation?

3. Can you change your status in any way once you have entered into the New Covenant?

4. In Hebrews 6:16 the writer stated an "oath confirms what is said and puts an end to all argument." What did God do to end all arguments concerning your status with him?

Because God wanted to make the unchanging nature of his purpose very clear to the heirs of what was promised, he confirmed it with an oath. God did this so that, by two unchangeable things in which it is impossible for God to lie, we who have fled to take hold of the hope set before us may be greatly encouraged.

Hebrews 6:17, 18

5. How does the following verse encourage you in times of trials and tribulations?

For I am convinced that nothing ... will be able to separate us from the love of God that is in Christ Jesus our Lord.

Romans 8:38, 39

PROMISE #3

"...they will all know me."

Hebrews 8:11

1. How does Jesus define eternal life?

Now this is eternal life: that they may know you, the only true God, and Jesus Christ, whom you have sent.

John 17:3

2. What kind of knowing does Jesus mean – a factual knowledge about God or a relationship with God?

My prayer is not for them alone. I pray also for those who will believe in me through their message, that all of them may be one, Father, just as you are in me and I am in you.

John 17:20, 21

3. According to this passage, how does the Holy Spirit enable you
to experience this personal knowledge of Jesus?

*"But when he, the Spirit of truth, comes, he will guide you into all
truth. He will not speak on his own; he will speak only what he hears,
and he will tell you what is yet to come. He will bring glory to me
by taking from what is mine and making it known to you. All that
belongs to the Father is mine. That is why I said the Spirit will take
from what is mine and make it known to you."*

John 16:13-15

PROMISE #4

I will forgive their wickedness and will remember their sins no more.
Hebrews 8:12

1. Since the New Covenant is now in effect, are your sins forgiven?

2. What does the statement "God remembers your sins no more"
mean to you?

3. Do you need to provide some kind of symbolic sacrifice to enable this in your life?

   And where these have been forgiven, there is no longer any sacrifice for sin.

   Hebrews 10:18

4. What does this mean with regard to Jesus as your high priest?

   Such a high priest meets our need—one who is holy, blameless, pure, set apart from sinners, exalted above the heavens. Unlike the other high priests, he does not need to offer sacrifices day after day, first for his own sins, and then for the sins of the people. He sacrificed for their sins once for all when he offered himself.

   Hebrews 7:26, 27

5. In the New Covenant, do you look forward to forgiveness or do you rest in the forgiveness already provided?

   For he has rescued us from the dominion of darkness and brought us into the kingdom of the Son he loves, in whom we have redemption, the forgiveness of sins.

   Colossians 1:13, 14

Think about what this means

If you are in Christ, you are a beneficiary of the New Covenant!

This New Covenant is altogether better than the Old. Why would you ever want to live under the Old when the New beckons with such benefits to everyone!

WHAT ABOUT THE GENTILES?

Is the New Covenant just for Israel? You might think so if you read Jeremiah 31 and Hebrews 8. However, God's Word tells a different story.

1. What did God tell Hosea?

> *Yet the Israelites will be like the sand on the seashore, which cannot be measured or counted. In the place where it was said to them, 'You are not my people,' they will be called "sons of the living God."*
>
> Hosea 1:10

> *I will say to those called "Not my people," "You are my people"; and they will say, "You are my God."*
>
> Hosea 2:23

2. How did Paul interpret these passages?

> *What if he did this to make the riches of his glory known to the objects of his mercy, whom he prepared in advance for glory—even us, whom he also called, not only from the Jews but also from the Gentiles?*
>
> Romans 9:23, 24

3. What was God's purpose in instituting the New Covenant?

> *His purpose was to create in himself one new man out of the two, thus making peace, and in this one body to reconcile both of them to God through the cross, by which he put to death their hostility.*
>
> Ephesians 2:15b, 16

4. Based on these promises, are you in the New Covenant?

TAKE A REST

Without Jesus, the Old and New Covenants are meaningless and devoid of power. With Jesus, you can relate to both covenants properly. You can see the beauty of the Old even while you acknowledge that it could never bring you life. You can see the overwhelming power and glory of the New and rest in Jesus' finished work.

1. What does this mean for you?

> *The Spirit himself testifies with our spirit that we are God's children. Now if we are children, then we are heirs—heirs of God and co-heirs with Christ, if indeed we share in his sufferings in order that we may also share in his glory.*
>
> Romans 8:16, 17

2. According to the following passage, what is available to a New Covenant believer?

    There remains, then, a Sabbath-rest for the people of God; for anyone who enters God's rest also rests from his own work, just as God did from his.

    Hebrews 4:9, 10

3. From what work did God rest originally?

    By the seventh day God had finished the work he had been doing; so on the seventh day he rested from all his work.

    Genesis 2:2

4. From what work did Jesus rest?

    The point of what we are saying is this: We do have such a high priest, who sat down at the right hand of the throne of the Majesty in heaven.

    Hebrews 8:1

5. Did Joshua provide this kind of rest for Israel?

    For if Joshua had given them rest, God would not have spoken later about another day. There remains, then, a Sabbath-rest for the people of God.

    Hebrews 4:8, 9

6. How do you enter this rest?

For anyone who enters God's rest also rests from his own work, just as God did from his.

Hebrews 4:10

This rest is not a one-day-per-week shadow but the 24/7 reality of letting Jesus work in and through you what he already accomplished for you.

You are forgiven. Your sins have been taken away once and for all. You can enjoy a personal, intimate relationship with God. You belong. You are one of God's people and nothing can take that away. You have God's desires written on your heart in your mind. All this because of Jesus' work. There is nothing for you to do except rest in God's provision.

CHAPTER THREE

Our New High Priest – The Guarantee of the Will

In Chapters 1 and 2 we looked at an overview of the New Covenant. We learned about four astonishing promises. What are they?

Promise 1:

Promise 2:

Promise 3:

Promise 4:

How do you really know they are true and valid for today? Who can guarantee such incredible promises?

The answer to these questions should be obvious: Jesus! Jesus is the most important person in the history of the world. For example, enter the word "Jesus" into Google and you will get more than 200,000,000 hits. These links range from the ridiculous (Jesus costumes for Halloween) to the sublime (sites dedicated to praising our Lord and Savior). There are many sites offering "proof" that Jesus is **not** who he claimed to be. These sites attempt to debunk Christ's claims, or they offer the most profane language and graphics for the sole purpose of dragging him down to the basest human level. Regardless of one's point of view, no one can claim that Jesus was a non-event. He impacted the world as no one before or since has done.

THE REAL JESUS

So, who is Jesus? What did he claim about himself? What did others claim about him? If these claims are true, what are their ramifications? Why should we care?

1. Who were his parents?

> *So Joseph also went up from the town of Nazareth in Galilee to Judea, to Bethlehem the town of David, because he belonged to the house and line of David. He went there to register with Mary, who was pledged to be married to him and was expecting a child.*
>
> Luke 2:4, 5

2. When was he born?

> *In those days Caesar Augustus issued a decree that a census should be taken of the entire Roman world. (This was the first census that took place while Quirinius was governor of Syria.)*
>
> Luke 2:1, 2

Think about what this means

The history of Augustus Caesar is well-documented. He reigned for 45 years, from about 31 BC (after defeating Marc Antony and Cleopatra) until his death in 14 AD. This time period was considered to be Rome's golden age.

Though less well-known, Quirinius really existed and really did serve as governor of Syria. He was reported, both by Josephus and an inscription discovered in the city of Aleppo, to have managed the census called for by Augustus Caesar. He became governor of Syria, which included Palestine, in 6 BC.

Therefore, Jesus was born sometime between 6 BC and 4 BC (when King Herod the Great died).

3. Was he part of a larger family?

   "Isn't this the carpenter's son? Isn't his mother's name Mary, and aren't his brothers James, Joseph, Simon and Judas? Aren't all his sisters with us? Where then did this man get all these things?"

   Matthew 13:55, 56

4. When did Jesus die?

   Meanwhile Jesus stood before the governor, and the governor asked him, "Are you the king of the Jews?" "Yes, it is as you say," Jesus replied. When he was accused by the chief priests and the elders, he gave no answer. Then Pilate asked him, "Don't you hear the testimony they are bringing against you?

   Matthew 27:11-13

Think about what this means

Pontius Pilate was procurator of Judea from 26-36 AD. According to an inscription found at Caesarea, he commanded 500-1000 auxiliary troops. The best estimate of Jesus' death is sometime between 30 AD and 33 AD.

Although many, including liberal theologians, have attempted to "prove" that Jesus either never existed or was a relatively meaningless character, no evidence has been found that refutes the accounts given by Matthew, Mark and Luke. All the key places, events and people have historical support.

Therefore, you can conclude that Jesus really did exist. His humanity is not in question.

WHAT DID JESUS CLAIM ABOUT HIMSELF?

1. What did Jesus say to his parents when they found him in the temple?

   After three days they found him in the temple courts, sitting among the teachers, listening to them and asking them questions... "Why were you searching for me?" he asked. "Didn't you know I had to be in my Father's house?"

   Luke 2:46, 49

2. Jesus literally said, "I had to be in the things of my Father." What was he claiming about himself at the age of 12?

3. According to these four passages, what does Jesus claim about Himself?

    a. *"Before Abraham was born, I Am."*

    John 8:58

    b. *"I am in the Father and the Father is in Me..."*

    John 14:11

    c. *"I and the Father are one."*

    John 10:30

    d. *"I am he."* [The word "he" is added by most translations. Literally, Jesus said, "I AM."]

    John 18:5

4. What benefits do you have because of who Jesus is?

    a. *Then Jesus declared, "I am the bread of life. Whoever comes to me will never go hungry, and whoever believes in me will never be thirsty.*

John 6:35

    b. *When Jesus spoke again to the people, he said, "I am the light of the world. Whoever follows me will never walk in darkness, but will have the light of life."*

John 8:12

    c. *I am the gate; whoever enters through me will be saved. They will come in and go out, and find pasture.*

John 10:9

    d. *I am the good shepherd. The good shepherd lays down his life for the sheep.*

John 10:11

    e. *Jesus said to her, "I am the resurrection and the life. The one who believes in me will live, even though they die; and whoever lives by believing in me will never die. Do you believe this?"*

John 11:25, 26

    f. I am the true vine, and my Father is the gardener.

John 15:1

    g. Jesus answered, "I am the way and the truth and the life. No one comes to the Father except through me.

John 14:6

Think about what this means

Jesus regularly and boldly declared himself to be God. He was not the least bit reticent or apologetic about it. There is no other way to explain these claims except that Jesus meant them exactly as he said them.

Therefore, there is no middle ground. Jesus either is God, or he is not.

If Jesus is not God, then close this study guide and move on to something more meaningful.

If Jesus is God, then everything he claimed about himself is true. Your only possible response is to fall at his feet in adoration and praise.

OTHERS MADE CLAIMS ABOUT JESUS

In each of the following passages, who is speaking and what claim did he make?

> *In the beginning was the Word, and the Word was with God, and the Word was God. He was with God in the beginning. Through him all things were made; without him nothing was made that has been made. In him was life, and that life was the light of all mankind. The light shines in the darkness, and the darkness has not overcome it.*
>
> John 1:1-5

> *The Word became flesh and made his dwelling among us. We have seen his glory, the glory of the one and only Son, who came from the Father, full of grace and truth.*
>
> John 1:14

> *The next day John saw Jesus coming toward him and said, "Look, the Lamb of God, who takes away the sin of the world! This is the one I meant when I said, 'A man who comes after me has surpassed me because he was before me.'*
>
> John 1:29, 30

> *Simon Peter answered, "You are the Messiah, the Son of the living God."*
>
> Matthew 16:16

Thomas said to him, "My Lord and my God!"

John 20:28

He fell to the ground and heard a voice say to him, "Saul, Saul, why do you persecute me?" "Who are you, Lord?" Saul asked. "I am Jesus, whom you are persecuting," he replied. "Now get up and go into the city, and you will be told what you must do."

Acts 9:4-6

Think about what this means

John the Baptist fully believed he was God.

Jesus' disciples fully believed he was God, even when they did not understand why that was so important.

Even Saul of Tarsus recognized Jesus as God when confronted by him on the road to Damascus.

THE SUPERIORITY OF JESUS

Why should you care that Jesus is both human and divine?

1. How did God's method of communication with humanity change?

   In the past God spoke to our forefathers through the prophets at many times and in various ways, but in these last days he has spoken to us by his Son, whom he appointed heir of all things, and through whom he made the universe.

   Hebrews 1:1, 2

2. How does Jesus compare to Moses?

   Moses was faithful as a servant in all God's house, testifying to what would be said in the future. But Christ is faithful as a son over God's house.

   Hebrews 3:5, 6

3. How does Jesus compare to Aaron?

   For it is clear that our Lord descended from Judah, and in regard to that tribe Moses said nothing about priests. And what we have said is even more clear if another priest like Melchizedek appears, one who has become a priest not on the basis of a regulation as to his ancestry but on the basis of the power of an indestructible life.

   Hebrews 7:14-16

4. What did Jesus have to offer that Levitical priests did not?

Now there have been many of those priests, since death prevented them from continuing in office; but because Jesus lives forever, he has a permanent priesthood. Therefore he is able to save completely those who come to God through him, because he always lives to intercede for them.
Hebrews 7:23-25

5. What is another critically important difference between Jesus and Levitical priests?

The point of what we are saying is this: We do have such a high priest, who sat down at the right hand of the throne of the Majesty in heaven, and who serves in the sanctuary, the true tabernacle set up by the Lord, not by man.
Hebrews 8:1, 2

6. Because of Jesus, what has happened to the Old Covenant?

By calling this covenant "new," he has made the first one obsolete; and what is obsolete and aging will soon disappear.
Hebrews 8:13

7. What did Jesus provide that the Old Covenant could not provide?

He did not enter by means of the blood of goats and calves; but he entered the Most Holy Place once for all by his own blood, having obtained eternal redemption.
Hebrews 9:12

8. What was the difference between Jesus' sacrifice and all the Old Covenant sacrifices?

But when this priest had offered for all time one sacrifice for sins, he sat down at the right hand of God. Since that time he waits for his enemies to be made his footstool, because by one sacrifice he has made perfect forever those who are being made holy.

Hebrews 10:12-14

9. What is the result of Jesus' superiority?

Therefore, brothers, since we have confidence to enter the Most Holy Place by the blood of Jesus, by a new and living way opened for us through the curtain, that is, his body, and since we have a great priest over the house of God, let us draw near to God with a sincere heart in full assurance of faith.

Hebrews 10:19-22a

10. What is the Bible's encouragement to you in day to day life?

Let us fix our eyes on Jesus, the author and perfecter of our faith, who for the joy set before him endured the cross, scorning its shame, and sat down at the right hand of the throne of God. Consider him who endured such opposition from sinful men, so that you will not grow weary and lose heart.

Hebrews 12:2, 3

Jesus is fully human and fully divine. He completely fulfilled the Old Covenant. He is, by God's declaration, our Great High Priest.

This is why John was so careful to describe Jesus accurately in his first letter.

> *What was from the beginning, what we have heard, what we have seen with our eyes, what we have looked at and touched with our hands, concerning the Word of Life—and the life was manifested, and we have seen and testify and proclaim to you the eternal life, which was with the Father and was manifested to us—what we have seen and heard we proclaim to you also, so that you too may have fellowship with us; and indeed our fellowship is with the Father, and with His Son Jesus Christ. These things we write, so that our joy may be made complete.*
>
> 1 John 1:1-4

Jesus truly is the key to everything. With him, the Old Covenant was fulfilled and is now obsolete. With him, the New Covenant is a reality and you have direct access to God, based on the provisions stated by God himself.

Without Jesus, there is no hope. With Jesus, you are completely victorious, because Jesus has become the guarantee of a better covenant!

> *Because of this oath, Jesus has become the guarantor of a better covenant.*
>
> Hebrews 7:22

CHAPTER FOUR

The Legal Document – Is It Valid?

We've used the Bible to explain everything we've studied thus far, but can you trust it? Is it valid? How can you know it is reliable? In this chapter we will answer a few of the most common criticisms of the Bible and provide you with answers you can share with your family and friends.

The Bible is the most important source of truth you have. It is the book that introduces you to Jesus and tells you about the New Covenant. It is the book that reveals all you've been given for life and Godliness. If the Bible is not valid, then nothing concerning your beliefs is valid. It is no wonder that so many people, both inside and outside the church, have tried to explain it away.

We'll begin with three crucial testimonies regarding the Bible from Jesus, Paul and Peter. Then we'll talk about how to understand the Bible. Finally, we'll offer a very brief explanation of how the Bible came to us in its present form.

WHAT DID JESUS SAY ABOUT THE BIBLE?

First, we must realize that no one in Jesus' day called it the Bible. Usually, these writings were called the scrolls or the word of God. Our word "bible" actually comes from a Greek word that simply means "book".

1. What is truth?

    Sanctify them by the truth; your word is truth.

    John 17:17

Notice that Jesus identifies his own words with the "your word," that is, God's word.

2. Is truth temporary or eternal?

    Heaven and earth will pass away, but my words will never pass away.

    Matthew 24:35

3. If Jesus is God and the Bible is true, what is the result?

    To the Jews who had believed him, Jesus said, "If you hold to my teaching, you are really my disciples. Then you will know the truth, and the truth will set you free."

    John 8:31, 32

Think about what this means

Jesus clearly identified himself with the Bible, declaring his own words to have the same power and authority as the scriptures so familiar to his hearers. Further, he declared that the truth of God's word, Jesus' word, would set you free. Therefore, the question of biblical reliability, accuracy and authority is answered primarily on the basis of Jesus' divinity. If Jesus is not God, then the Bible is not God's word, is not true and has no authority in your life.

WHAT DID PAUL SAY ABOUT THE BIBLE?

All Scripture is God-breathed and is useful for teaching, rebuking, correcting and training in righteousness, so that the man of God may be thoroughly equipped for every good work.

2 Timothy 3:16, 17

1. Is the Bible inspired in part or altogether?

2. What is the Bible's purpose?

3. What will this accomplish for you?

WHAT DID PETER SAY ABOUT THE BIBLE?

1. How valuable were the Old Testament prophets to Peter?

   And we have the word of the prophets made more certain, and you will do well to pay attention to it, as to a light shining in a dark place, until the day dawns and the morning star rises in your hearts. Above all, you must understand that no prophecy of Scripture came about by the prophet's own interpretation. For prophecy never had its origin in the will of man, but men spoke from God as they were carried along by the Holy Spirit.

   2 Peter 1:19-21

2. Who compelled the Old Testament prophets to write?

3. What made the word of the prophets more certain?

   We did not follow cleverly invented stories when we told you about the power and coming of our Lord Jesus Christ, but we were eyewitnesses of his majesty. For he received honor and glory from God the Father when the voice came to him from the Majestic Glory, saying, "This is my Son, whom I love; with him I am well pleased." We ourselves heard this voice that came from heaven when we were with him on the sacred mountain.

   2 Peter 1:16-18

Think about what this means

Peter understood, beyond all doubt, that Jesus is God. Therefore, the entire Old Testament was confirmed by Jesus and met its fulfillment **in** Jesus.

4. According to Peter, what is the power of the word of God?

For you have been born again, not of perishable seed, but of imperishable, through the living and enduring word of God. For, "All men are like grass, and all their glory is like the flowers of the field; the grass withers and the flowers fall, but the word of the Lord stands forever." And this is the word that was preached to you.

1 Peter 1:23-25

But the Counselor, the Holy Spirit, whom the Father will send in my name, will teach you all things and will remind you of everything I have said to you.

John 14:26

Think about what this means

The same weight of authenticity and authority is given to the apostles' words and writings as any Old Testament writing. This is why the gospels, history, letters and Revelation were collected together to create the New Testament.

HOW YOU CAN UNDERSTAND THE BIBLE

God's truth marches through the Hebrew scripture, our Old Testament, reaches its fulfillment in Jesus himself, and then is given to the entire world in the form of the collected writings of the apostles in our New Testament.

> *However, as it is written: "No eye has seen, no ear has heard, no mind has conceived what God has prepared for those who love him"—but God has revealed it to us by his Spirit. The Spirit searches all things, even the deep things of God. For who among men knows the thoughts of a man except the man's spirit within him? In the same way no one knows the thoughts of God except the Spirit of God. We have not received the spirit of the world but the Spirit who is from God, that we may understand what God has freely given us. This is what we speak, not in words taught us by human wisdom but in words taught by the Spirit, expressing spiritual truths in spiritual words. The man without the Spirit does not accept the things that come from the Spirit of God, for they are foolishness to him, and he cannot understand them, because they are spiritually discerned. The spiritual man makes judgments about all things, but he himself is not subject to any man's judgment: "For who has known the mind of the Lord that he may instruct him?" But we have the mind of Christ.*
>
> 1 Corinthians 2:9-16

1. Who reveals what God has prepared for you?

2. What does the Spirit do?

3. Can you know the thoughts of God?

4. Who does?

5. Which spirit have you received?

6. Why?

7. Is human wisdom enough?

8. Can a person without the Holy Spirit accept what the Spirit gives?

9. Why?

10. Can a person without the Holy Spirit understand what the Spirit gives?

11. Why?

12. What is the result of having the Holy Spirit?

13. What does it really mean to have the Holy Spirit?

14. Based on this passage, who is your teacher?

15. As you trust the Holy Spirit to teach you the meaning of the Word, to whom is He pointing you to?

> *You study the Scriptures diligently because you think that in them you have eternal life. These are the very Scriptures that testify about me, yet you refuse to come to me to have life.*
>
> John 5:39, 40 (emphasis added)

A SHORT HISTORY OF THE BIBLE

How did the Bible come to be as we know it today? (This information is taken from Wilmington's Bible Handbook, 1997, Tyndale House Publishers).

By 300 B.C. (at the latest) all the Old Testament books had been written, collected, revered, and recognized as official, canonical books. We know, from the Bible itself, that the books of Moses were stored beside the Ark of the Covenant in the Most Holy Place.

> *After Moses finished writing in a book the words of this law from beginning to end, he gave this command to the Levites who carried the ark of the covenant of the Lord: "Take this Book of the Law and place it beside the ark of the covenant of the Lord your God. There it will remain as a witness against you.*
>
> Deuteronomy 31:24-26

The existing Old Testament books were taken to Babylon, because Daniel had access to them.

> *In the first year of his reign, I, Daniel, understood from the Scriptures, according to the word of the Lord given to Jeremiah the prophet, that the desolation of Jerusalem would last seventy years.*
>
> Daniel 9:2

Ezra apparently brought those books back to Jerusalem and read the Law to the people when the temple was completed.

> *All the people assembled as one man in the square before the Water Gate. They told Ezra the scribe to bring out the Book of the Law of Moses, which the Lord had commanded for Israel.*
>
> Nehemiah 8:1

During the Third Council of Carthage, A.D. 397, the 27 books that make up the NT as we know it were declared to be canonical.

These gospels, letters, etc. were unwelcome at the temple in Jerusalem, so they were preserved within the Christian community by various local churches. This is why Paul could refer to other letters being read.

However, this collection of 39 Old Testament and 27 New Testament books are not "official" because various committees decided they should be "official" but because they already were authentic. The Council of Carthage used this logic:

- *Authorship.* Was the author respected and regarded as speaking with divine authority?
- *Local church acceptance.* Had it been read by the various churches? What was their opinion of it?
- *Early church leaders' recognition.* Did the students of Christ's apostles (such as Polycarp, a disciple of John) quote from the letter?
- *Content.* What did the book teach? Did it contradict other recognized books?
- *Personal edification.* Did the book inspire, convict, and edify local congregations and individual believers?

In other words, the various writings were authentic because they were inspired by God. The job of the committees was to discover God's communication, not to define His communication.

The various authors were God's mouthpiece. They literally spoke for God. This is why authorship trumps all the other logic. If they were speaking for God, it doesn't matter whether local churches accepted the words.

As we saw above in Peter's claims regarding God's word, Jesus Himself is the One who confirmed the Old Testament prophets' words. This is echoed by the writer to the Hebrews.

If the words themselves are not enough, note that no other book in the history of the world has been as closely studied as the Bible.

> *"Even though the original books are lost, there is overwhelming evidence that our translated Bibles today represent amazingly accurate copies of the first manuscripts. The number of existing Hebrew and Greek Bible manuscript fragments runs literally into the thousands. There are some 5,300 [New Testament] Greek manuscripts. Years of scholarly comparison among these manuscripts have led to a consensus among scholars that the Bible as we have it today is virtually identical to the original manuscripts."* (Willmington, H. L. (1997). Willmington's Bible handbook (p. 881). Wheaton, IL: Tyndale House Publishers.)

No other historical book can match this!

The Bible truly is God's word to us. It can be trusted to be our sole basis of faith and practice. It is about Jesus from beginning to end. It is consistent. It is powerful.

However, because the Bible is a spiritual book, it can be understood only if revealed by the Holy Spirit. Thankfully, Jesus promised that the Holy Spirit would do this, and this is exactly what he does.

Remember, the Bible is God's testimony concerning Jesus. "You diligently study the Scriptures because you think that by them you possess eternal life. These are the Scriptures that testify about me, yet you refuse to come to me to have life." (John 5:39-40).

Jesus is the beginning and end of scripture, its unifying theme.

CHAPTER FIVE

The Death of the One – Christ's Finished Work on the Cross

"When I was 15 years old I stole money from a teacher at school. No one ever caught me, but I've been consumed with guilt over this ever since. Can God forgive me? Does he hate me? Am I lost?"

If you're being honest with yourself right now you probably have asked very similar questions. What happens when you blow it? Have you lost fellowship with God?

The first three parts of our study laid the foundation for what is to come. Now it is time to take a deeper look at several details. The first detail we will explore is Jesus' death on the cross. Why was it necessary? What did it accomplish? Is there any more to be accomplished?

THE SIN PROBLEM

How did sin enter the world? What is its result?

1. What warning did God give to Adam regarding the Tree of the Knowledge of Good and Evil?

   And the Lord God commanded the man, "You are free to eat from any tree in the garden; but you must not eat from the tree of the knowledge of good and evil, for when you eat of it you will surely die."

   Genesis 2:16, 17

2. How did Eve explain God's warning to the serpent?

   The woman said to the serpent, "We may eat fruit from the trees in the garden, but God did say, 'You must not eat fruit from the tree that is in the middle of the garden, and you must not touch it, or you will die.'"

   Genesis 3:2, 3

3. Did both Adam and Eve understand that death would be the consequence?

4. How did the serpent sow doubt in Eve's mind?

   "You will not surely die," the serpent said to the woman. "For God knows that when you eat of it your eyes will be opened, and you will be like God, knowing good and evil."

   Genesis 3:4, 5

5. What was the result of this conversation?

When the woman saw that the fruit of the tree was good for food and pleasing to the eye, and also desirable for gaining wisdom, she took some and ate it. She also gave some to her husband, who was with her, and he ate it.

Genesis 3:6

6. What happened when they ate the fruit?

Then the eyes of both of them were opened, and they realized they were naked; so they sewed fig leaves together and made coverings for themselves.

Genesis 3:7

7. Did they die physically?

Think about what this means

It is interesting that Satan told just enough truth to make his lies more palatable. They did not die immediately, their eyes were opened, and they became like God, knowing good and evil.

And the Lord God said, "The man has now become like one of us, knowing good and evil. He must not be allowed to reach out his hand and take also from the tree of life and eat, and live forever."

Genesis 3:22

But they lost their relationship with God when the Lord God banished them from Eden and they were prevented from eating from the Tree of Life. Therefore, they died spiritually at the moment and physically eventually. God indeed told the truth. Sin drove a wedge of separation between God and humanity.

8. What did God reveal about His plan for humanity?

So the Lord God said to the serpent ... "I will put enmity between you and the woman, and between your offspring and hers; he will crush your head, and you will strike his heel."

Genesis 3:14, 15

Think about what this means

This was God's first statement of a plan to rescue us.

9. What was the result of Adam and Eve's disobedience?

Therefore, just as sin entered the world through one man, and death through sin, and in this way death came to all men, because all sinned...

Romans 5:12

10. According to the verse above, how did their choice impact you?

11. How does the Psalmist describe the condition of man apart from God?

> *The fool says in his heart, "There is no God." They are corrupt, their deeds are vile; there is no one who does good. The Lord looks down from heaven on the sons of men to see if there are any who understand, any who seek God. All have turned aside, they have together become corrupt; there is no one who does good, not even one.*
>
> Psalm 14:1-3

12. How does Paul describe this situation?

> *As for you, you were dead in your transgressions and sins, in which you used to live when you followed the ways of this world and of the ruler of the kingdom of the air, the spirit who is now at work in those who are disobedient. All of us also lived among them at one time, gratifying the cravings of our sinful nature and following its desires and thoughts. Like the rest, we were by nature objects of wrath.*
>
> Ephesians 2:1-3

Think about what this means

Your problem is that you are dead, just as God told Adam it would be. You need life, but life is impossible as long as sin is part of the equation. You are helpless. There is nothing you can do by or for yourself to remedy the problem. Someone else must deal with this; someone must destroy this wedge that separates you from God.

WHAT DID JESUS' DEATH ACCOMPLISH?

Anyone who has a passing familiarity with Christianity knows that Jesus died for our sins. But what does that mean?

1. What did the prophet Isaiah say would happen regarding sin?

   Yet it was the Lord's will to crush him and cause him to suffer, and though the Lord makes his life a guilt offering, he will see his offspring and prolong his days, and the will of the Lord will prosper in his hand. After the suffering of his soul, he will see the light of life and be satisfied; by his knowledge my righteous servant will justify many, and he will bear their iniquities. Therefore I will give him a portion among the great, and he will divide the spoils with the strong, because he poured out his life unto death, and was numbered with the transgressors. For he bore the sin of many, and made intercession for the transgressors.

   Isaiah 53:10-12

2. Did Jesus understand God's will?

   Going a little farther, he fell with his face to the ground and prayed, "My Father, if it is possible, may this cup be taken from me. Yet not as I will, but as you will."

   Matthew 26:39; also verses 42 and 43

3. Could the sacrifices commanded in the Mosaic Covenant take away sins?

   ...because it is impossible for the blood of bulls and goats to take away sins.

   Hebrews 10:4

4. What was so different about Jesus?

*Day after day every priest stands and performs his religious duties;
again and again he offers the same sacrifices, which can never take
away sins. But when this priest had offered for all time one sacrifice
for sins, he sat down at the right hand of God, and since that time he
waits for his enemies to be made his footstool. For by one sacrifice he has
made perfect forever those who are being made holy.*

Hebrews 10:11-14

5. What did Jesus' death accomplish?

*But now he has appeared once for all at the end of the ages to do away
with sin by the sacrifice of himself.*

Hebrews 9:26b

6. What does this mean to you?

*All this is from God, who reconciled us to himself through Christ and
gave us the ministry of reconciliation: that God was reconciling the
world to himself in Christ, not counting men's sins against them.*

2 Corinthians 5:18, 19a

7. What does it mean to you that God is not counting your sins
against you?

ONCE FOR ALL

There is nothing more that needs to be accomplished relative to the sin problem. Jesus' death is enough.

1. Who took Jesus' life?

    The reason my Father loves me is that I lay down my life—only to take it up again. No one takes it from me, but I lay it down of my own accord. I have authority to lay it down and authority to take it up again. This command I received from my Father."

    John 10:17, 18

2. What does this suggest about your involvement in God's plan?

3. Did Jesus think he completed the task?

    Later, knowing that all was now completed, and so that the Scripture would be fulfilled, Jesus said, "I am thirsty." A jar of wine vinegar was there, so they soaked a sponge in it, put the sponge on a stalk of the hyssop plant, and lifted it to Jesus' lips. When he had received the drink, Jesus said, "It is finished." With that, he bowed his head and gave up his spirit.

    John 19:28-30

4. Will Jesus ever again deal with sin?

...so Christ was sacrificed once to take away the sins of many people; and he will appear a second time, not to bear sin, but to bring salvation to those who are waiting for him.

Hebrews 9:28

FORGIVENESS IS MINE

1. What do you have in Jesus?

In him we have redemption through his blood, the forgiveness of sins.

Ephesians 1:7a

2. Could this be possible without Jesus' death?

In fact, the law requires that nearly everything be cleansed with blood, and without the shedding of blood there is no forgiveness.

Hebrews 9:22

3. What else did Jesus' death provide for you?

For if, when we were God's enemies, we were reconciled to him through the death of his Son...

Romans 5:10a

4. Is this forgiveness a future event, or has it already occurred?

I write to you, dear children, because your sins have been forgiven on account of his name.

1 John 2:12

5. How many of your sins were forgiven in Jesus?

When you were dead in your sins and in the uncircumcision of your sinful nature, God made you alive with Christ. He forgave us all our sins...

Colossians 2:13

6. Have you believed in Jesus? If so, what have have you received?

All the prophets testify about him that everyone who believes in him receives forgiveness of sins through his name.

Acts 10:43

Jesus took on the greatest rescue mission of all time. Adam and Eve committed spiritual suicide, for themselves and for all of us, but God, in Christ, said, "I will not leave them without hope." Jesus lived a sinless life and died a perfect death, and by doing so he solved the sin problem once and for all.

Jesus obliterated the wedge of separation between you and God. In Him, you are a forgiven person.

CHAPTER SIX

New Life – Experiencing the Power of the Resurrection Here and Now

Jesus' victory over sin provided reconciliation and forgiveness. This was absolutely essential to bridging the gulf that existed between God and us, but it was only the first half of God's total solution. God wasn't done with his miracle of grace. He had something more for you.

That something more is resurrection life. The good news is that Jesus is alive. In this chapter, you will discover why this is good news for you.

IT'S ABOUT LIFE

The resurrection of Jesus Christ is the single most important event in human history. His resurrection has significance for you today. Let's find out why.

1. How did Jesus describe his mission?

   The thief comes only to steal and kill and destroy; I have come that they may have life, and have it to the full.

   John 10:10

2. What kind of life was Jesus talking about?

   For God so loved the world that he gave his one and only Son, that whoever believes in him shall not perish but have eternal life.

   John 3:16

3. Why did John write his gospel?

   But these are written that you may believe that Jesus is the Christ, the Son of God, and that by believing you may have life in his name.

   John 20:31

4. What is your problem according to this passage?

   As for you, you were dead in your transgressions and sins, in which you used to live when you followed the ways of this world and of the ruler of the kingdom of the air, the spirit who is now at work in those who are disobedient. All of us also lived among them at one time, gratifying the cravings of our sinful nature and following its desires and thoughts. Like the rest, we were by nature objects of wrath.

Ephesians 2:1-3

5. How does the resurrection of Jesus Christ address this problem?

6. What did Jesus do at the Father's command relative to his death?

The reason my Father loves me is that I lay down my life—only to take it up again. No one takes it from me, but I lay it down of my own accord. I have authority to lay it down and authority to take it up again. This command I received from my Father.

John 10:17, 18

7. For Jesus to offer this eternal life he had to be alive. What was the eyewitness testimony concerning this?

…and that he appeared to Peter, and then to the Twelve. After that, he appeared to more than five hundred of the brothers at the same time, most of whom are still living, though some have fallen asleep. Then he appeared to James, then to all the apostles, and last of all he appeared to me also, as to one abnormally born.

1 Corinthians 15:5-8

8. What is the gospel that saves?

> *Now, brothers, I want to remind you of the gospel I preached to you, which you received and on which you have taken your stand. By this gospel you are saved, if you hold firmly to the word I preached to you. Otherwise, you have believed in vain. For what I received I passed on to you as of first importance: that Christ died for our sins according to the Scriptures, that he was buried, that he was raised on the third day according to the Scriptures...*
>
> 1 Corinthians 15:1-4

Think about what this means

Jesus' resurrection proved that he was victorious over death. Sin could not defeat him and death could not hold him. In this single event Jesus undid everything that Satan had tried to do in order to ruin humanity and all creation.

FROM DEATH TO LIFE

You knew you needed forgiveness, but as you've learned in this study your real problem is that you need life. How do you get that life?

1. What is the result of Jesus' death, burial and resurrection?

> *For if, when we were God's enemies, we were reconciled to him through the death of his Son, how much more, having been reconciled, shall we be saved through his life!*
>
> Romans 5:10

2. How do you get this life?

But what does it say? "The word is near you; it is in your mouth and in your heart," that is, the word of faith we are proclaiming: That if you confess with your mouth, "Jesus is Lord," and believe in your heart that God raised him from the dead, you will be saved. For it is with your heart that you believe and are justified, and it is with your mouth that you confess and are saved.

Romans 10:8-10

3. What happens when you confess Jesus as Lord?

I tell you the truth, whoever hears my word and believes him who sent me has eternal life and will not be condemned; he has crossed over from death to life.

John 5:24

4. How does Jesus describe this process of crossing over from death to life?

Jesus replied, "Very truly I tell you, no one can see the kingdom of God unless they are born again.

John 3:3

5. How did Paul describe this process?

But because of his great love for us, God, who is rich in mercy, made us alive with Christ even when we were dead in transgressions—it is by grace you have been saved.

Ephesians 2:4, 5

THE GIFT

Not only does God make you alive in Christ, he also gives to you his Spirit. Paul describes this as "Christ in you, the hope of glory." Colossians 1:27.

1. Why was it good for Jesus to leave?

   Now I am going to him who sent me, yet none of you asks me, "Where are you going?" Because I have said these things, you are filled with grief. But I tell you the truth: It is for your good that I am going away. Unless I go away, the Counselor will not come to you; but if I go, I will send him to you.

   John 16:5-7

2. When did the Holy Spirit come?

   When the day of Pentecost came, they were all together in one place. Suddenly a sound like the blowing of a violent wind came from heaven and filled the whole house where they were sitting. They saw what seemed to be tongues of fire that separated and came to rest on each of them. All of them were filled with the Holy Spirit and began to speak in other tongues as the Spirit enabled them.

   Acts 2:1-4

3. How did Paul describe this reality?

   You, however, are controlled not by the [flesh] but by the Spirit, if the Spirit of God lives in you. And if anyone does not have the Spirit of Christ, he does not belong to Christ. But if Christ is in you, your body is dead because of sin, yet your spirit is alive because of righteousness.

And if the Spirit of him who raised Jesus from the dead is living in you, he who raised Christ from the dead will also give life to your mortal bodies through his Spirit, who lives in you.

Romans 8:9-11

4. Who came to live inside of you when you trusted Christ?

   He redeemed us in order that the blessing given to Abraham might come to the Gentiles through Christ Jesus, so that by faith we might receive the promise of the Spirit.

Galatians 3:14

ABSOLUTE CERTAINTY

God wants you to know, beyond any doubt, that you are saved. He hasn't left this to chance.

1. Can you know you have eternal life?

   He who has the Son has life; he who does not have the Son of God does not have life. I write these things to you who believe in the name of the Son of God so that you may know that you have eternal life.

1 John 5:12, 13

2. How do you know?

   Anyone who believes in the Son of God has this testimony in his heart. Anyone who does not believe God has made him out to be a liar, because he has not believed the testimony God has given about his Son. And this is the testimony: God has given us eternal life, and this life is in his Son.

   1 John 5:10, 11

3. Who is the primary source of this testimony?

   The Spirit himself testifies with our spirit that we are God's children.

   Romans 8:16

4. Can you lose this life?

   My sheep listen to my voice; I know them, and they follow me. I give them eternal life, and they shall never perish; no one can snatch them out of my hand. My Father, who has given them to me, is greater than all; no one can snatch them out of my Father's hand. I and the Father are one.

   John 10:27-30

5. What are you called now that you have eternal life?

   How great is the love the Father has lavished on us, that we should be called children of God! And that is what we are!

   1 John 3:1a

6. Why is Jesus' resurrection so important to us? What would be the case if Jesus was not raised?

For if the dead are not raised, then Christ has not been raised either. And if Christ has not been raised, your faith is futile; you are still in your sins. Then those also who have fallen asleep in Christ are lost. If only for this life we have hope in Christ, we are to be pitied more than all men.

1 Corinthians 15:16-19

Jesus' resurrection is the second half of the solution. You needed someone to solve the sin problem, and Jesus did that by dying for you. But more than that, you needed someone to give you life again. Jesus did that by the power of his resurrection from the dead.

Now, both forgiveness and eternal life are available in him. Both are free gifts of grace. Neither can be earned. Once accepted, neither can be lost.

Life Application

1. Have you thought of yourself as spiritually dead? Or did you think you were neutral, neither dead nor alive, and in control of your own destiny?

2. Have your sins kept you from accepting the life offered in Jesus because of your unworthiness?

3. Are you willing to let go of everything that is holding you back in order to receive the life and forgiveness freely offered in Jesus?

CHAPTER SEVEN

Shadow and Reality – Law and Grace

God's initiative on your behalf truly is amazing! He could have given you what you deserved. Instead, he reached out of eternity and into time to save you.

Now that you have been saved, how should you live?

The next three parts of our study will deal with your response to God's initiative. In this chapter we will look at law and grace. What is law? What is its purpose? What is grace? Why is grace better than law? When you answer these questions you will know how to live.

The New Testament is clear. Just as you were saved by grace through faith, you are to live by grace through faith. Paul put it this way in Galatians 3:25, "Now that faith has come, we are no longer under the supervision of the law."

WHAT IS LAW?

The Hebrew word torah means "instruction, direction and law." It is used in the sense of the entire Law. It refers to the laws, ordinances, commands, decrees and requirements of the Lord found in Exodus, Leviticus and Numbers. In addition, it is used of the entire book of Deuteronomy, Moses' exposition of the Torah. (See Baker, W., & Carpenter, E. E. (2003). The complete word study dictionary: Old Testament (1220). Chattanooga, TN: AMG Publishers.)

The Greek word *nomos* means "what is proper." For the most part, when used in the New Testament it refers to the Pentateuch, the first five books of the Bible, but sometimes it refers to the entire Old Testament.

Usually, we define the word "holy" as righteous with regard to the law, but the word "holy" does not mean righteous. It means "set apart." Only in the context of God does "holy" take on a spiritual meaning, and it does so only because God, by his very nature and essence, is eternally "set apart." He is flawless, sinless and perfect. He is not us.

1. What does God demand in the law?

   I am the Lord who brought you up out of Egypt to be your God; therefore be holy, because I am holy.

   Leviticus 11:45

2. According to the law, what is the penalty for sin?

   The soul who sins is the one who will die.

   Ezekiel 18:20a

3. What is the law's purpose?

   Now we know that whatever the law says, it says to those who are under the law, so that every mouth may be silenced and the whole world held accountable to God. Therefore no one will be declared righteous in his sight by observing the law; rather, through the law we become conscious of sin.

   Romans 3:19, 20

4. Did this purpose have an end?

   So the Law was our guardian until Christ came that we might be justified by faith.

   Galatians 3:24 (NIV 2011)

5. According to this verse, does the law play a role in your life as a believer?

   Now that this faith has come we are no longer under a guardian.

   Galatians 3:25

THE TRUTH ABOUT THE LAW

1. What are three things the law cannot do?

   a. *...that a man is not justified by observing the law, but by faith in Jesus Christ.*

   Galatians 2:16a

b. *I do not set aside the grace of God, for if righteousness could be gained through the law, Christ died for nothing!*

Galatians 2:21

c. *Is the law, therefore, opposed to the promises of God? Absolutely not! For if a law had been given that could impart life, then righteousness would certainly have come by the law.*

Galatians 3:21

2. What are three things the law actually does?

a. *For when we were controlled by the [flesh], the sinful passions aroused by the law were at work in our bodies, so that we bore fruit for death.*

Romans 7:5

b *Now if the ministry that brought death, which was engraved in letters on stone, came with glory, so that the Israelites could not look steadily at the face of Moses because of its glory, fading though it was, will not the ministry of the Spirit be even more glorious? If the ministry that condemns men is glorious, how much more glorious is the ministry that brings righteousness!*

2 Corinthians 3:7-9

c. *All who rely on observing the law are under a curse, for it is written: "Cursed is everyone who does not continue to do everything written in the Book of the Law."*

Galatians 3:10

3. How is the Old Covenant law described in the following passage?

The law is only a shadow of the good things that are coming—not the realities themselves. For this reason it can never, by the same sacrifices repeated endlessly year after year, make perfect those who draw near to worship.

Hebrews 10:1

JESUS AND THE LAW

1. Was Jesus under the law?

But when the time had fully come, God sent his Son, born of a woman, born under law, to redeem those under law, that we might receive the full rights of sons.

Galatians 4:4, 5

2. Did Jesus teach the law?

You have heard that it was said, "Do not commit adultery." But I tell you that anyone who looks at a woman lustfully has already committed adultery with her in his heart. If your right eye causes you to sin, gouge it out and throw it away.

Matthew 5:27-29a

3. Did Jesus finish the law?

   Christ is the end of the law so that there may be righteousness for everyone who believes.

   Romans 10:4

4. What did Jesus do for you relative to the law?

   Christ redeemed us from the curse of the law by becoming a curse for us, for it is written: "Cursed is everyone who is hung on a tree." He redeemed us in order that the blessing given to Abraham might come to the Gentiles through Christ Jesus, so that by faith we might receive the promise of the Spirit.

   Galatians 3:13, 14

5. Are the Ten Commandments part of this law?

   Now if the ministry that brought death, which was engraved in letters on stone, came with glory, so that the Israelites could not look steadily at the face of Moses because of its glory, fading though it was, will not the ministry of the Spirit be even more glorious?

   2 Corinthians 3:7-8

6. So, since Jesus fulfilled the law and redeemed you from the law, how are you to live?

   So I say, live by the Spirit, and you will not gratify the desires of the flesh. For the flesh desires what is contrary to the Spirit, and the Spirit what is contrary to the flesh. They are in conflict with each other, so that you do not do what you want. But if you are led by the Spirit, you are not under law.

   Galatians 5:16-18 (NIV 2011)

7. What does it mean to live by the Spirit?

> *For the grace of God that brings salvation has appeared to all men. It teaches us to say "No" to ungodliness and worldly passions, and to live self-controlled, upright and godly lives in this present age, while we wait for the blessed hope—the glorious appearing of our great God and Savior, Jesus Christ, who gave himself for us to redeem us from all wickedness and to purify for himself a people that are his very own, eager to do what is good.*
>
> Titus 2:11-14

THE TRUTH ABOUT GRACE

You may have grown up with a definition of grace that went something like this: Grace is God's unmerited favor towards us; or as an acrostic – **G**od's **R**iches **A**t **C**hrist's **E**xpense. Both of these capture a very small part of the total picture.

1. Who finishes the work begun in you?

> *…being confident of this, that he who began a good work in you will carry it on to completion until the day of Christ Jesus.*
>
> Philippians 1:6

2. In reality, who works in you?

> *Therefore, my dear friends, as you have always obeyed—not only in my presence, but now much more in my absence—continue to work out your salvation with fear and trembling, for it is God who works in you to will and to act according to his good purpose.*
>
> Philippians 2:12, 13

Grace is not a "what". Grace is a "who" – God himself living in you via the Holy Spirit. To live by grace is to be led by the Spirit of God.

3. Why is grace better than law?

   a. *...for all have sinned and fall short of the glory of God, and are justified freely by his grace through the redemption that came by Christ Jesus.*

   Romans 3:23, 24

   b. *...so that, just as sin reigned in death, so also grace might reign through righteousness to bring eternal life through Jesus Christ our Lord.*

   Romans 5:21

c. *We have different gifts, according to the grace given us. If a man's gift is prophesying, let him use it in proportion to his faith.*

Romans 12:6

d. *But he said to me, "My grace is sufficient for you, for my power is made perfect in weakness." Therefore I will boast all the more gladly about my weaknesses, so that Christ's power may rest on me.*

2 Corinthians 12:9

e. *For it is by grace you have been saved, through faith—and this not from yourselves, it is the gift of God...*

Ephesians 2:8

f. *But we see Jesus, who was made a little lower than the angels, now crowned with glory and honor because he suffered death, so that by the grace of God he might taste death for everyone.*

Hebrews 2:9

4. What happens when you try to use law and grace together?

    a. *Neither do men pour new wine into old wineskins. If they do, the skins will burst, the wine will run out and the wineskins will be ruined. No, they pour new wine into new wineskins, and both are preserved.*

                      Matthew 9:17

    b. *And if by grace, then it is no longer by works; if it were, grace would no longer be grace.*

                      Romans 11:6

    c. *You foolish Galatians! Who has bewitched you? Before your very eyes Jesus Christ was clearly portrayed as crucified. I would like to learn just one thing from you: Did you receive the Spirit by observing the law, or by believing what you heard? Are you so foolish? After beginning with the Spirit, are you now trying to attain your goal by human effort?*

                      Galatians 3:1-3

    d. *I am astonished that you are so quickly deserting the one who called you by the grace of Christ and are turning to a different gospel—which is really no gospel at all.*

                      Galatians 1:6, 7a

In short, grace is the opposite of law. Instead of shutting your mouth in shame, by grace you open it to praise Jesus. Grace provides everything law cannot. Grace overpowers the law. Why? Because grace is Jesus himself, living in you by his Holy Spirit.

Here is a working definition of grace: *"Grace is the empowering Presence of God enabling you to be who God created you to be, and to do what He has called you to do."* (James Ryle)

5. What should you do with regard to the law?

   For through the law I died to the law so that I might live for God.
                                                       Galatians 2:19

6. What is the result?

   For sin shall not be your master, because you are not under law, but under grace.
                                                       Romans 6:14

7. How then should you live?

   I have been crucified with Christ and I no longer live, but Christ lives in me. The life I now live in the body, I live by faith in the Son of God, who loved me and gave himself for me.
                                                       Galatians 2:20

Life Application

1. Is there anything you must do to earn God's approval?

2. Is there anything you can offer him as "proof" of your fitness for salvation?

3. Have you been trying to live up to the standards of the law in order to convince yourself or others that you really are a Christian?

4. Are you willing to die to the law and come alive in Jesus?

Law has only one thing to say to you: You are doomed! Without Jesus you are held captive by the Law of Sin and Death.

On the other hand, Grace shouts, "Saved!" In Jesus there is no longer any condemnation, because the Law of the Spirit of Life has set you free from the Law of Sin and Death (see Romans 8:1-4).

Jesus made this possible. He, alone, fulfilled the law. He fulfilled it on your behalf, just like he died and rose from the dead on your behalf. He has been relentless in his pursuit of you, in his initiation of forgiveness and salvation to you.

Grace is internal. Law is external. Grace is the reality represented by the law's shadow. If you do not live in the reality of grace you must live in the shadow world of law.

You have been given a clear choice – law or Grace. Choose grace!

CHAPTER EIGHT

God's People – Our New Identity in Christ

Who are you? Are you a parent, a CEO, a student, a doctor? Are you an alcoholic, a drug abuser, a sex addict? There is nothing more sinister about the world's system than what it says regarding your identity. In every advertisement, every television show, every movie, every song, every political appeal there is at least one lie concerning identity, at least one appeal to a need that should be fulfilled if you're "normal".

This is done solely because it works. The economy, the ways in which you seek advancement on the job, how you educate yourself – in fact, almost everything you do is driven by what you believe about yourself. If a company can convince you that you can be someone different with their product or service, then they have you right where they want you.

In this chapter we will look at your identity. Are you going to let the world dictate your behavior, or will you hold on to the truth explained in God's word?

THE OLD YOU

1. In whose image did God make Adam and Eve?

    Then God said, "Let us make mankind in our image, in our likeness, so that they may rule over the fish in the sea and the birds in the sky, over the livestock and all the wild animals, and over all the creatures that move along the ground."

    Genesis 1:26

2. Whose image did Seth bear?

    When Adam had lived 130 years, he had a son in his own likeness, in his own image; and he named him Seth.

    Genesis 5:3

3. What does this mean?

    Therefore, just as sin entered the world through one man, and death through sin, and in this way death came to all men, because all sinned...

    Romans 5:12

4. As a result of Adam's sin, what identity did you inherit?

> *...Through the disobedience of one man, many were made sinners.*
> Romans 5:19a

5. To whom did Jesus direct his ministry?

> *On hearing this, Jesus said to them, "It is not the healthy who need a doctor, but the sick. I have not come to call the righteous, but sinners."*
> Mark 2:17

6. What did Jesus come into the world to do?

> *Here is a trustworthy saying that deserves full acceptance: Christ Jesus came into the world to save sinners – of whom I am the worst.*
> 1 Timothy 1:15

7. What happens when Jesus saves a sinner?

> *In the same way, I tell you, there is rejoicing in the presence of the angels of God over one sinner who repents."*
> Luke 15:10

IMAGE IS EVERYTHING

Understanding your true identity is life-changing!

1. Whose image does God intend for you to have?

   When God created man, he made him in the likeness of God.

   Genesis 5:1

2. What has God decreed in this regard?

   For those God foreknew he also predestined to be conformed to the likeness of his Son, that he might be the firstborn among many brothers.

   Romans 8:29

4. What does this verse say about the image Jesus bears?

   The Son is the image of the invisible God, the firstborn over all creation.

   Colossians 1:15

5. According to this verse, when you receive Christ what do you become?

   Yet to all who received him, to those who believed in his name, he gave the right to become children of God.

   John 1:12

6. What gives you this right?

    ...children born not of natural descent, nor of human decision or a husband's will, but born of God.

    John 1:13

7. According to John, what is necessary for a change of identity?

    Jesus replied, "Very truly I tell you, no one can see the kingdom of God unless they are born again.

    John 3:3

A NEW NAME

1. What happens at the moment of salvation?

    Therefore, if anyone is in Christ, he is a new creation; the old has gone, the new has come!

    2 Corinthians 5:17

2. How does God make this change of identity in you?

    Because you are sons, God sent the Spirit of his Son into our hearts, the Spirit who calls out, "Abba, Father."

    Galatians 4:6

3. What name is given to you when you are saved?

> *...because those who are led by the Spirit of God are sons of God. For you did not receive a spirit that makes you a slave again to fear, but you received the Spirit of sonship. And by him we cry, "Abba, Father." The Spirit himself testifies with our spirit that we are God's children.*
>
> Romans 8:15, 16

BENEFITS OF BEING A CHILD OF GOD

1. From what have you been delivered?

> *For you were once darkness, but now you are light in the Lord.*
>
> Ephesians 5:8a

2. As a child of God, what have you become?

> *Now if we are children, then we are heirs—heirs of God and co-heirs with Christ, if indeed we share in his sufferings in order that we may also share in his glory.*
>
> Romans 8:17

3. Where is your citizenship?

> *But our citizenship is in heaven. And we eagerly await a Savior from there, the Lord Jesus Christ...*
>
> Philippians 3:20

4. How complete is your identification with Jesus?

...for all of you who were baptized into Christ have clothed yourselves with Christ.

Galatians 3:27

5. How safe is your life?

For you died, and your life is now hidden with Christ in God. When Christ, who is your life, appears, then you also will appear with him in glory.

Colossians 3:3, 4

ATTACKS ON OUR IDENTITY

1. What do you know about yourself after salvation?

But you were washed, you were sanctified, you were justified in the name of the Lord Jesus Christ and by the Spirit of our God.

1 Corinthians 6:11b

2. How does Satan attack your new identity?

Who will bring any charge against those whom God has chosen? It is God who justifies. Who is he that condemns? Christ Jesus, who died— more than that, who was raised to life—is at the right hand of God and is also interceding for us.

Romans 8:33, 34

3. How does Paul describe this situation?

> *For the flesh desires what is contrary to the Spirit, and the Spirit what is contrary to the flesh. They are in conflict with each other, so that you do not do what you want.*
>
> Galatians 5:17 (NIV 2011)

5. How do these attacks reveal themselves:

- In your family?

- In your job?

- At school?

- In advertising of all types?

- At church?

HOW TO OVERCOME ATTACKS ON YOUR IDENTITY

1. What does the Holy Spirit do for you?

> *In the same way, the Spirit helps us in our weakness. We do not know what we ought to pray for, but the Spirit himself intercedes for us with groans that words cannot express.*
>
> Romans 8:26

2. What does God do for you?

   And we know that in all things God works for the good of those who love him, who have been called according to his purpose.

   Romans 8:28

3. When you are attacked, what can you rely on?

   What, then, shall we say in response to this? If God is for us, who can be against us?

   Romans 8:31

4. In spite of these attacks, what does Jesus promise you?

   No, in all these things we are more than conquerors through him who loved us.

   Romans 8:37

5. Why can you overcome Satan's attacks?

   For I am convinced that neither death nor life, neither angels nor demons, neither the present nor the future, nor any powers, neither height nor depth, nor anything else in all creation, will be able to separate us from the love of God that is in Christ Jesus our Lord.

   Romans 8:38, 39

HOW TO LIVE IN THIS NEW IDENTITY

1. Has God given you a spirit of fear?

   For you did not receive a spirit that makes you a slave again to fear, but you received the Spirit of sonship.

   Romans 8:15a

2. What else have you received from God?

   We have this hope as an anchor for the soul, firm and secure. It enters the inner sanctuary behind the curtain, where Jesus, who went before us, has entered on our behalf.

   Hebrews 6:19, 20a

3. How should you respond to these gifts?

   Therefore, I urge you, brothers, in view of God's mercy, to offer your bodies as living sacrifices, holy and pleasing to God—this is your spiritual act of worship.

   Romans 12:1

4. What will be the result of that response?

   Do not conform any longer to the pattern of this world, but be transformed by the renewing of your mind. Then you will be able to test and approve what God's will is—his good, pleasing and perfect will.

   Romans 12:2

Life Application

1. What proof do you have of God's love?

   How great is the love the Father has lavished on us, that we should be called children of God! And that is what we are!

   1 John 3:1a

2. Are you willing to allow God's declaration about you change you from the inside out?

Tragically, some believe that having a terrible identity (alcoholic, loser, unlovable, etc.) is better than having no identity at all. This attitude shows a complete lack of understanding regarding God's overwhelming love and grace. Yes, you were born dead spiritually, condemned to an eternity separated from God. You were a sinner by nature. But all that changed!

God reached down to you and gave you eternal life and forgiveness in Jesus. By accepting that gift, you were given the only identity that matters, the only identity that never can be taken away from you.

Welcome to real life, fellow Child of God!

CHAPTER NINE

New Covenant Life – Faith, Hope and Love
PART ONE

So far, we've looked at the New Covenant, Jesus, the Bible and Jesus' complete victory over sin and death. These explain God's amazing initiative on your behalf. He could have spoken you out of existence. Instead, he reached out of eternity and into time in order to save you.

Then we began a deeper look at what your response should be to God's initiative. We saw the superiority of grace over law, proof that God himself will finish what he started in you! And we demonstrated the power of your new identity—Child of God.

In these final two chapters we will put all the pieces together. Your life is to be rooted in faith, hope and love. These great themes bring you back to the God who started it all.

FAITH

Faith means "to win over, persuade. Subjectively meaning firm persuasion, conviction, belief in the truth, veracity, reality or faithfulness (though rare). Objectively meaning that which is believed, doctrine, the received articles of faith." (Zodhiates)

1. How does the Bible define faith?

   Now faith is being sure of what we hope for and certain of what we do not see.

   Hebrews 11:1

2. Based on the following verses, what are some of the things you cannot see?

   a. *It is because of him that you are in Christ Jesus, who has become for us wisdom from God—that is, our righteousness, holiness and redemption.*

   1 Corinthians 1:30

   b. *Not only is this so, but we also rejoice in God through our Lord Jesus Christ, through whom we have now received reconciliation.*

   Romans 5:11

   c. *When you were dead in your sins and in the uncircumcision of your sinful nature, God made you alive with Christ. He forgave us all our sins...*

   Colossians 2:13

3. Since you cannot see those things of which you are certain, how do you exercise faith?

   Let us fix our eyes on Jesus, the author and perfecter of our faith, who for the joy set before him endured the cross, scorning its shame, and sat down at the right hand of the throne of God. Consider him who endured such opposition from sinful men, so that you will not grow weary and lose heart.

   Hebrews 12:2, 3

4. What assurance does faith provide according to these passages?

   a. *I write these things to you who believe in the name of the Son of God so that you may know that you have eternal life.*

   1 John 5:13

   b. *This is the confidence we have in approaching God: that if we ask anything according to his will, he hears us.*

   1 John 5:14

   c. *And if we know that he hears us—whatever we ask—we know that we have what we asked of him.*

   1 John 5:15

d. *We know that anyone born of God does not continue to sin; the one who was born of God keeps him safe, and the evil one cannot harm him.*

1 John 5:18

e. *We know that we are children of God, and that the whole world is under the control of the evil one.*

1 John 5:19

f. *We know also that the Son of God has come and has given us understanding, so that we may know him who is true.*

1 John 5:20a

g. *And we are in him who is true—even in his Son Jesus Christ. He is the true God and eternal life.*

1 John 5:20b

HOPE

Hope is defined as the "desire of some good with expectation of obtaining it." (Zodhiates) *This "expectation of obtaining it" is the difference between hope as experienced by a lost person and hope as experienced by a child of God.*

1. Based on the following passages, what does your hope in Christ guarantee?

   a. *Then Paul, knowing that some of them were Sadducees and the others Pharisees, called out in the Sanhedrin, "My brothers, I am a Pharisee, the son of a Pharisee. I stand on trial because of my hope in the resurrection of the dead."*

   Acts 23:6

   b. *...through whom we have gained access by faith into this grace in which we now stand. And we rejoice in the hope of the glory of God.*

   Romans 5:2

   c. *For the creation was subjected to frustration, not by its own choice, but by the will of the one who subjected it, in hope that the creation itself will be liberated from its bondage to decay and brought into the freedom and glory of the children of God.*

   Romans 8:20, 21

d. *To them God has chosen to make known among the Gentiles the glorious riches of this mystery, which is Christ in you, the hope of glory.*

Colossians 1:27

e. *Brothers, we do not want you to be ignorant about those who fall asleep, or to grieve like the rest of men, who have no hope. We believe that Jesus died and rose again and so we believe that God will bring with Jesus those who have fallen asleep in him.*

1 Thessalonians 4:13, 14

f. *Paul, a servant of God and an apostle of Jesus Christ for the faith of God's elect and the knowledge of the truth that leads to godliness—a faith and knowledge resting on the hope of eternal life...*

Titus 1:1, 2a

2. What do all of these things have in common? Have you obtained any of these yet?

3. Why do we have the expectation of obtaining these things?

> *And you also were included in Christ when you heard the word of truth, the gospel of your salvation. Having believed, you were marked in him with a seal, the promised Holy Spirit, who is a deposit guaranteeing our inheritance until the redemption of those who are God's possession—to the praise of his glory.*
>
> Ephesians 1:13, 14

4. Based on this verse, why is hope significant to you today?

> *...because we have heard of your faith in Christ Jesus and of the love you have for all God's people—the faith and love that spring from the hope stored up for you in heaven and about which you have already heard in the true message of the gospel.*
>
> Colossians 1:4, 5

Think about what this means

Your hope is based solely on the person and work of Jesus. As you saw in previous chapters, Jesus took care of sin once and for all and provided the way to eternal life. But it doesn't stop there. Your future is guaranteed by Jesus. He is God Almighty. He is coming again. He is going to recreate the universe. And he gave you the Holy Spirit to prove that his promise is a guarantee, a statement of fact.

LOVE

We've mentioned God's love several times throughout these studies, but we haven't taken the time to define it. We are talking about the Greek word agápē. It is defined as "God's willful direction toward man. It involves God doing what He knows is best for man and not necessarily what man desires." (Zodhiates) What does this "direction" look like? How does it play out in your life?

1. What does this passage teach you about God's nature?

   Dear friends, let us love one another, for love comes from God. Everyone who loves has been born of God and knows God. Whoever does not love does not know God, because God is love.

   1 John 4:7, 8

2. What are the characteristics of God's love?

   Love is patient, love is kind. It does not envy, it does not boast, it is not proud. It is not rude, it is not self-seeking, it is not easily angered, it keeps no record of wrongs. Love does not delight in evil but rejoices with the truth. It always protects, always trusts, always hopes, always perseveres.

   1 Corinthians 13:4-7

3. What are some ways God displayed this love for you?

   a. *For God so loved the world that he gave his one and only Son, that whoever believes in him shall not perish but have eternal life.*

   John 3:16

b. *But God demonstrates his own love for us in this: While we were still sinners, Christ died for us.*

Romans 5:8

c. *In love he predestined us to be adopted as his sons through Jesus Christ, in accordance with his pleasure and will…*

Ephesians 1:5

d. *But because of his great love for us, God, who is rich in mercy, made us alive with Christ even when we were dead in transgressions—it is by grace you have been saved.*

Ephesians 2:4, 5

e. *How great is the love the Father has lavished on us, that we should be called children of God!*

1 John 3:1a

f. *This is love: not that we loved God, but that he loved us and sent his Son as a [propitiation] for our sins.*

1 John 4:10

4. What did God's patience mean to Paul?

But for that very reason I was shown mercy so that in me, the worst of sinners, Christ Jesus might display his immense patience as an example for those who would believe in him and receive eternal life.

1 Timothy 1:16

5. What does God's patience mean to you?

Bear in mind that our Lord's patience means salvation, just as our dear brother Paul also wrote you with the wisdom that God gave him.

2 Peter 3:15

6. Kindness is an act that is useful or beneficial to the recipient. How did God express his kindness to you?

But when the kindness and love of God our Savior appeared, he saved us, not because of righteous things we had done, but because of his mercy. He saved us through the washing of rebirth and renewal by the Holy Spirit...

Titus 3:4, 5

7. In light of God's great love for you, what kind of life has he called you to?

A new command I give you: Love one another. As I have loved you, so you must love one another.

John 13:34

How can you live a life of love?

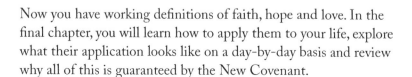

Now you have working definitions of faith, hope and love. In the final chapter, you will learn how to apply them to your life, explore what their application looks like on a day-by-day basis and review why all of this is guaranteed by the New Covenant.

CHAPTER TEN

New Covenant Life – Faith, Hope and Love
PART TWO

In the previous chapter we explored definitions of faith, hope and love.

In this final chapter we will put all the pieces together. Your life is to be rooted in faith, hope and love. These great themes bring you back to the God who started it all.

APPLYING FAITH, HOPE AND LOVE

1. How much of the Christian life can you do yourself?

   I am the vine; you are the branches. If a man remains in me and I in him, he will bear much fruit; apart from me you can do nothing.
   John 15:5

2. Who is the source of the Christian life?

3. What attitude will result from the truth that Jesus is the vine?

   Going a little farther, he fell with his face to the ground and prayed, "My Father, if it is possible, may this cup be taken from me. Yet not as I will, but as you will."

   Matthew 26:39

4. How did Peter explain it?

   To this you were called, because Christ suffered for you, leaving you an example, that you should follow in his steps. "He committed no sin, and no deceit was found in his mouth." When they hurled their insults at him, he did not retaliate; when he suffered, he made no threats. Instead, he entrusted himself to him who judges justly.

   1 Peter 2:21-23

5. What did Jesus say about love?

   As the Father has loved me, so have I loved you. Now remain in my love.

   John 15:9

6. What did Paul say about love?

   For Christ's love compels us, because we are convinced that one died for all, and therefore all died.

   2 Corinthians 5:14

THE CHRIST LIFE IN ACTION

Paul made a stunning statement in his letter to the Galatians. "The only thing that counts" is how he began. That should grab your attention. What follows is the key to experiencing life to the full. It is "faith expressing itself through love."

1. How does faith express itself through love in this passage?

    Get rid of all bitterness, rage and anger, brawling and slander, along with every form of malice. Be kind and compassionate to one another, forgiving each other, just as in Christ God forgave you.

    Ephesians 4:31, 32

2. How does faith in Christ enable you to handle difficult circumstances?

    Rejoice in the Lord always. I will say it again: Rejoice… Do not be anxious about anything, but in everything, by prayer and petition, with thanksgiving, present your requests to God.

    Philippians 4:4, 6

3. What is God's promise to you?

    And we know that in all things God works for the good of those who love him, who have been called according to his purpose.

    Romans 8:28

4. What have you forgotten if you are struggling with the love of God?

For if you possess these qualities in increasing measure, they will keep you from being ineffective and unproductive in your knowledge of our Lord Jesus Christ. But if anyone does not have them, he is nearsighted and blind, and has forgotten that he has been cleansed from his past sins.

2 Peter 1:8, 9

5. What did Paul pray for you?

I pray that out of his glorious riches he may strengthen you with power through his Spirit in your inner being, so that Christ may dwell in your hearts through faith. And I pray that you, being rooted and established in love, may have power, together with all the saints, to grasp how wide and long and high and deep is the love of Christ, and to know this love that surpasses knowledge—that you may be filled to the measure of all the fullness of God.

Ephesians 3:16-19

6. How is this love made complete in you?

Dear friends, since God so loved us, we also ought to love one another. No one has ever seen God; but if we love one another, God lives in us and his love is made complete in us.

1 John 4:11, 12

Living the Christian life is not hard, it is impossible. If faith, hope and love were anything other than based completely on the overwhelming victory of Jesus you would be crushed.

But Jesus was and is victorious, and he has given you his victory. You can live with complete assurance. You can experience a changed life and a renewed mind. You will be conformed to his image.

Every part of the Bible – whether explaining the beginning of things, the history of Israel, the successes and failures of various people, the present or the future – is about Jesus. He is everything you need, literally. He has given you everything you need, literally. If you will fix your eyes on him you will see where to walk and what to do.

This is the promise of God, and he confirmed it with an oath. Because God cannot lie you can rest, truly rest, for time and eternity.

NEW COVENANT LIFE

One final time, let's take another look at the four magnificent promises in the New Covenant. What are they?

This is the covenant I will make with the house of Israel after that time, declares the Lord. I will put my laws in their minds and write them on their hearts. I will be their God, and they will be my people. No longer will a man teach his neighbor, or a man his brother, saying, 'Know the Lord,' because they will all know me, from the least of them to the greatest. For I will forgive their wickedness and will remember their sins no more."

Hebrews 8:10-12

• "I will put My laws…

• "I will be their God…

- "No longer will they teach...

- "For I will forgive...

1. When God talked about "laws" was he thinking of the Mosaic Law?

   For when there is a change of the priesthood, there must also be a change of the law.

   Hebrews 7:12

2. What laws was he thinking of?

   And this is his command: to believe in the name of his Son, Jesus Christ, and to love one another as he commanded us.

   1 John 3:23

3. How do these laws manifest themselves in our lives?

   And now these three remain: faith, hope and love. But the greatest of these is love.

   1 Corinthians 13:13

So, we've come full-circle back to the beginning. God, in his unlimited love and grace, was unwilling for you to remain lost. He provided everything you need for salvation in Jesus. You have only to accept Jesus and everything is yours. And when you accept him, he will make sure that faith, hope and love – the New Covenant Life – is worked through you until you overflow to others. This is your assurance and your guarantee. This is your Jesus!

Simple Gospel, Simply Grace
How Your Christian Life is Really Supposed to Work

"We're all natural-born legalists," says author Bob Christopher. "We try to live for God, but it's impossible to do."

Why? Because all our efforts and ideas are based on the same fear-based, guilt-driven plot line: Try harder. As you've undoubtedly noticed, it just doesn't work.

Simple Gospel, Simply Grace showcases an alternative, which is actually God's original plan: Everything you're trying to achieve in the Christian life has already been given to you—from God, by grace, in Christ.

Do you struggle to receive what God has freely given? How can you begin to experience true freedom, assurance of your forgiveness, and victory over sin? How can the power that raised Jesus from the dead enable you to live and love the way He did?

You'll discover the answers in this crystal-clear portrayal of the simple gospel—which is simply grace.

simplegospelsimplygrace.com

"Bob Christopher humbly and powerfully points us to Jesus Christ as our source of purpose and fulfillment. If you've been longing to lean into the love of Jesus, Simply Grace is one of those exceptional books that truly delivers. You don't want to miss this one."

Andrew Farley, bestselling author of The Naked Gospel and pastor.

andrewfarley.org

Made in the USA
Monee, IL
11 March 2021

61661765R00066